BLANK

Jake Wild Hall is one half of ᵍ
Club and winner of the PBH 2016 Spirit Of The Free Fringe Award.
He has performed on BBC Radio and at festivals and literary events
across the UK, including touring his debut pamphlet *Solomon's
World*—longlisted for Best Pamphlet in the 2018 Saboteur Awards.
He co-edited anthologies *The Dizziness of Freedom* and *Alter Egos*
(Bad Betty Press, 2018 and 2019).

Blank

Published by Bad Betty Press in 2019
www.badbettypress.com

Cover design by Amy Acre

Printed and bound in the United Kingdom

A CIP record of this book is available from the British Library.

ISBN: 978-1-913268-00-8

BLANK

PRESS

The Christians gave me comic books, as if I would be scared of burning in Hell while I was already there.

– Kimya Dawson

Blank

To Amy and Rory

Contents

Hymn

this is the longest my nails have been
in relation to my anxiety

i paint them joy & relief
hope my life will reflect them
it does
i am too lucky to be melancholy
too in love for that
two new footsteps in my house
posting too many books tweeting too many things joy on my
instagram story dad jokes on my facebook

you are in bed painting your toenails
& hoping for breath

my child asks me to replicate her joy
so i read books & switch to cartoons when my family calls
i wonder how many more times it will not be bad news
how loud i will play the cartoons when it is
i don't leave the house i am worried i will get the call in public
both me & my daughter crying in the ball pit

soon i will call my mum & she will be so sad i can't be strong for her
soon my uncle will break
soon my grandmother who i didn't know could will freeze over
she will not be the woman i grew up with
who would be

soon your siblings will carry you
soon the relatives will see each other when it's not christmas or
a wedding
soon you will leave a widow
no matter how many times we say we are lucky for the time we
have had
it will be too soon
it is always too soon

When It Happens

it will be a friday
nothing extraordinary
except it will happen
you will drink until
sunday then be sober
& cry like there
is nothing to lose
there won't be

Original Pirate Material

we stand still for the picture
big looking for land hoping he can save them from the rocks
middle asleep at the wheel steering into the wind
little walking the plank with no fear
captain behind the camera steady in the storm
i am still absent too often little firefly in my hand gratification
calculator dopamine drip
but we are working things out
middle & little
smiling running laughing
we are too normal
that is fine

This Morning is a Biscuit Dunked into Fresh Tea

your staccato breaths are a green light
the atoms between us go silent

is it possible i am the same person who last night
stood under the skylight watching the sky fall
in bass bass snare

the things i have been avoiding
turn to ulcers in my mouth

There Are Many Types of Love

we write lists & draw star charts & hold ourselves up to them for
approval

food coming to the door is just something that happens
like breathing or phone screens

we drown ourselves & pray for october
october is a traitor though it stands at the crossroads with a
crashed car & no apology

london is the world until it sings all the wrong hymns
in your church

an angel grows in your room
at night her halo wakes the house
when she finally rests you know the difficulty setting of this
game is hope

Normal is Such a Boring Word

everything said whilst holding a basket of freshly baked bread is a question mark to you anyway

cleaning is therapy when it's the only time you have to yourself

i'm not doing very well at selling this bread i'm holding would you like some?

i've been remembering all my dreams again but not sharing them with anyone

it's like having more feelings

this bread is going stale i think it might be ok if you toast it

heat is a cure for most things

however temporary it is it is always above average

i guess i can share my dreams with you

i keep killing people by mistake

i always wonder in how many of my lives i have killed myself

Sláinte Gan Slaghdán agus Bás ná n'Dairbhre

i hope i do here
surrounded by ocean
breathing in time with the waves

here that is as beautiful as hope
here that is as quiet as the unmarked stones
here that is rich in rebellion

i hope it is here

Kin

after the war
we are still silver birch
a little more shine
catching fire from
the embers still

when you're watered
in gasoline
a change in season
can destroy a forest

You Are Grieving at the Bar

have been for 922 days straight
glass of brave face denial chaser

i see your reflection at the bottom of my glass too

two weeks ago we held each other & cried
it's the most natural thing we have done in years

last week i held your partner in my arms while she cried
i have not known how to reconcile our relationship since

i know how hard it is to remember a parent
at the moment you are forgetting both of mine

there is a storm in my stomach every time i think of you

The Time You Followed Your Bag through a Window Asking for Help in a Language All of Us Understand but None of Us Speak

they gave you an option
there is only one correct answer for

we discuss this pills still hidden
twenty-four years later

i have made a home of your sofa
i talk to myself in that same language

neither of our moons can be full
we acknowledge everything with silence

we don't look after anything in the present
we will fix it all once it's broken

Blank

blank
wake up
fall asleep
blank
pick it up
put it down
i shouldn't
but why
you're missing the point
blank
back to the start
when was the start
i am losing my days
it's fine
no it's not
blank
roll
then again
fine
then again
try this
it has no effect
blank
sleep is cause & effect
blank
it has no effect
no more relief
maybe this is the end

roll
blank
roll
then again
fine
then again
try this
it has no effect
blank
wake up
fall asleep
blank
pick it up
put it down
i shouldn't
but why
you're missing the point
blank
sleep is cause & effect
blank
back to the start
when was the start
i am losing my days
it's fine
no it's not
blank
it has no effect
no more relief
maybe this is the end

the first time you feel this it will be
infinite
not in a good way
your day will drag like fingernails on chalkboards
you will ask yourself why the sun in a clear sky is ugly
the morning will be an itch you can't scratch
human contact a necessity
the sun will go down
stars will come out
the heavens will be empty
at this point you will in one way or another start again

It's a 12-Week Course

when your body is a crash because you must not

when your brain is a protest & your skull a kettle

when your thoughts become voices when the voices become
continuous only saying jump or swallow

when you roll the burning bush into the sheets of your
abridged bible every morning so the holy ghost can pass
through you

when you are drunk on the sympathetic hum of the fridge

when the clock face is set to laconic

when waking is all you remember

when everyone is out to get you partner mum friends they are
all in on it & for no reason

when all of this becomes you

find yourself twelve deep to a room full of skin itch
coffee sip

take a deep breath kid

you're nearly there

Notes

'Sláinte Gan Slaghdán agus Bás ná n'Dairbhre' is an Irish toast meaning, 'May you have good health without illness, and die on Valentia.'

Acknowledgements

Some of these poems previously appeared in the *Anti-Hate Anthology* (Spoken Word London, 2019), *The Dizziness of Freedom* (Bad Betty Press, 2018) and on the Sugar & Dread podcast.

Thank you to everyone who has and continues to help me get better. And to Amy Acre for everything.

Other titles by Bad Betty Press

Solomon's World
Jake Wild Hall

Unremember
Joel Auterson

In My Arms
Setareh Ebrahimi

The Story Is
Kate B Hall

The Dizziness Of Freedom
Edited by Amy Acre
and Jake Wild Hall

I'm Shocked
Iris Colomb

Ode to Laura Smith
Aischa Daughtery

The Pale Fox
Katie Metcalfe

TIGER
Rebecca Tamás

The Death of a Clown
Tom Bland

While I Yet Live
Gboyega Odubanjo

Raft
Anne Gill

She Too Is a Sailor
Antonia Jade King

And They Are Covered in Gold Light
Amy Acre

Forthcoming:
No Weakeners
Tim Wells

Alter Egos
Edited by Amy Acre
and Jake Wild Hall

Lightning Source UK Ltd.
Milton Keynes UK
UKHW012134050719
345653UK00001B/113/P